To my dea

Thankyou for all
you do.

Love,

Sarah B
2022

Over
My
Shoulder

Sarah B Marsh-Rebelo

For my family who are my 'everything,' and my brother Raymond who forever has a corner of my heart. This journey is to honour the memory of my Mother because there is no other way, and for my Father who taught me the importance of never giving up.

There is a new voice on the literary horizon, and a most welcome voice it is. With a quality of expression that moves emotion from poet to reader without the cumbersome mediation of thought, Over My Shoulder *displays a burning passion of volcanic heat that burns away all that is not essential, leaving a small, flawless gem. Dark and sad and triumphant,* Over My Shoulder *is a love letter to life.*

-Richard Platt

Author of *As One Devil to Another: A Fiendish Correspondence in the Tradition of C. S. Lewis' The Screwtape Letters.*

A poet invites you into her home. She serves you tea, and as she stands to stoke a fire, the room fills with phantoms substantial as dark branches. Sarah Marsh-Rebelo, in this debut collection of poems, gives voice and grace to those phantoms. Over My Shoulder *is a lament for a lost family in which a mother somehow escapes her daughter and leaves her alone to find her place in the world. Beautifully told through a lyric sequence, it is not unlike the Gaelic fairy tale* Maid of the Waves, *in which a mermaid has her very essence stripped from her as she becomes human and births a family then one day flees back to the sea. In* Over My Shoulder, *one feels the singer of these lyrics to be forever torn between land and sea, presence and absence, body and being, and the lament she sings will move you, will haunt you.*

-*Poet Laureate* Sandra Alcosser

Author of *"Except by Nature"* and *"A Fish to Feed all Hunger."*

*No one who has a chance to hear Sarah Marsh-Rebelo
read her poems is likely to forget the music, the boldness,
the magnetism. And, so one is startled, when one reads the
lyrics that are half-whispers, over the shoulder, over the
years, bringing back the glimpse, the apparition. Why such
duality, one wonders? But then, one remembers that there
is duality in any real poet's voice: Argument with another
is rhetoric. Yeats taught us, argument with one's self is
poetry. One hears "tap,/tap, tap/ when a mind stirs" and
one knows there is an intimacy here in music, one finds it
also when "sparrows fly into the kitchen/overwhelming a
mind". This moment of intimacy where grieving is so
present is what I find unique.*

*There is wisdom in lines like "there is something
auspicious/about the moment/sunlight slices a room" or
poems such as "I Talk to Myself" and "It is Impossible
God is Close by When there is So Much Memory in the
World", "Listen to the Silence," and "From her Point of
View". Emily Dickinson told us that "after a great pain, a
formal feeling comes." And, reading the many poems of
pain in* Over My Shoulder *I asked myself: where is it, that
formal feeling? I think it is in these beautiful words: "In
her life/a woman is polished/ once or twice/like fine
silver./In these moments/she shimmers."*

-Ilya Kaminsky

Author of *Letters from Odessa:* Winner of the *Addison M.
Metcalf Award in Literature,* a *"Bunker Poetico"* award at
the Venice Bienial Festival in Italy, a *Ruth Lilly Poetry
Fellowship* and a *Lannan Foundation Literary Fellowship.*

*Marsh-Rebelo asks us to look at the world again, the way
our lives unravel like a story singing itself backward.
The narrative poems give us longing, aching, English
meadows ,the cracking of shells. "Feel life bend. Break
open the heart." "Dad found her naked...She'd told
him/she didn't like music in her clothes." "This poetry
gives us stories that split apart life."*

-Kate Gale

Author of *Fisher of Men* and *The Poet Divided* and
Founder of *Red Hen Press, Los Angeles, California.*

*Sarah Marsh-Rebelo sends us on a wrenching journey into
the heart. She carries the reader in and out of darkness.
Sometimes rough, then smooth—never failing to engage.
Read* Over My Shoulder *once for impact. Read it again for
understanding—and once more for deep nourishment.*

-Julie Maloney

Author of *Private Landscape* and Founder of *Women
Reading Aloud.*

*These are elegant, heartfelt poems. They welcome the
reader with directness and immediacy, and then deepen
and expand at each rereading.*

-Jerry Farber Ph.D

Renowned poet and essayist, Professor Jerry Farber is
author of the 1960's national best seller *The University as
Tomorrowland* which inspired nonviolent student protests
in late 1960's. *"The Student as Nigger,"* served as the title
essay of this book. His poem, *The Liberals' Song* became
the mantra for the Civil Rights Movement in 1963.

Acknowledgments

To John who supports my dreams with his unswerving love. With tremendous gratitude to Sandra Alcosser, Jane Hirshfield, Ilya Kaminsky, Steve Kowit, Kate Gale, Marilyn Chin, Jerry Farber, Joyce Gattas, Patricia Lee Lewis, Julie Maloney and Aron Suley, all of whom opened doors. To Valerie Hume who patiently listened. I treasure our friendship of thirty four years. With tremendous thanks to Rich Platt who encouraged me from the beginning saying, "Yes, you can" and to Austin Tipp for his gracious assistance with editing. The author gratefully thanks the publications in which some of these poems first appeared some in slightly different form: Perigee, Avocet, California Poets Anthology, The San Diego Poetry Review, San Diego Poetry Annual, 27 rue de fleures, The Women's Foundation Celebration, The New Jersey Times, and Foothill, a Journal of Poetry.

Contents

How surely gravity's law,
strong as an ocean current,
takes hold of even the smallest thing
and pulls it toward the heart of the world.

Rainer Maria Rilké

Lullaby for a Baby Falling

They lived several lives under the cloak of war,
nestled close at times, other times repenting. Tell me
about despair, yours, and I will tell you about theirs.

My father favoured wavy black hair,
mutton chop whiskers,
sailed in a fire engine over London at night.

When my mother was lonely she dug up the garden,
wrapped and unwrapped bulbs stored in newspapers
yellowed with age.

Early one morning as celandines bloomed
the air stirred in frenzy like wild bees before a storm.
Bombs burst! We ran along the path near our home.

The baby in my mother's stomach fell out too soon,
soaked her white uniform the color of blood.

She wrapped the blue baby,
laid her with care deep inside an old canvas bag.

We did not talk as we walked, her hand tight around mine.
When my father came home they fell into each other
as the walls of war closed in on their lives.

Nest

What is
that tap,
tap, tap?

An elegant shift
when
a mind stirs.

While empires
spiral toward
madness,

a woman
is kneading
her nest.

untangling
knots of her
own making.

Guns and the Dome

He caught snowflakes on his fingers, taught me
the purest taste on earth was snowflakes on my tongue.

Perhaps you've seen a city lined with fires,
one comes alive in that awful clarity.

Yells of firemen, screams in crackling flames,
every two minutes a new wave of planes.

The guns nearby sharp, far away muffled, a pause
of two minutes, night sky lit up in a pink, white glow.

As part of the 'war effort' hours stacked against him
my father helped put out flames in the dome of St. Paul's.

Three days later he drove into a Sunday morning.
The wooden steering wheel came off in his hands.

Those who understood must make way for those
who understand little, and at last nothing, nothing at all.

Dress Walks Out the Door

Hardly a day passes when I do not
think of her. It was summer in England.
She scraped dirt from her shoes,

dug carrots in stifling summer heat.
The stillness in the air could drive
a woman mad.

She slowly stirred soup in a yellow ceramic bowl,
tilted her head, wore a quiet smile.
When she was lonely sat by my side—

talked about war,
men who had forgotten their names,
slid her hand down her uniform

from the English Red Cross,
pinned medals on my dress.
Walked out the door.

Soft Curves

My mother gives birth, rides herself into screams.
London strips river veins, bridges fold like origami.
Someone listens, mouth open, nods his unshattered head.

It is night that concerns us, as if we just dreamt it.
Daylight floats ashes and jagged glass.
In shredded jackets coupon books curl at the edges.

My navy school beret sports a gold and green badge,
worn at an angle suggestive of French movies.
Gym slips sway to a rhythm gone wrong.

I discover soft curves, the new smell
of deep red. Learn the ritual of Irish nuns,
knuckles clenched like ivory balls.

A wooden ruler swishes down,
resembling the ancient statue of some religious rite,
smooth on the edges, worn well with time.

Rag and Bone

I sit silent in the bath as my mother throws up in the
porcelain sink. She sobs *If I'm pregnant I'll throw myself
under a train.*

Used and tired, filled up with time I wonder how she would
look flattened by a train, long chestnut hair
curled over the tracks.

Seven months later you burst into the world,
held your breath until you turned red.
In this life who of us is perfect?

From a second floor window we watch the rag
and bone man whip his grey horse as rain splatters
the streets.

Mum makes a game of looking for things she says, *we
don't need in this house anymore.* Cries when she sells him
leather bound books, books that lie open in every room.

From Mahler's Fourth Symphony she plays the last
movement. What breaking heart could play a child's vision
of heaven?

I curl up by the brass pedals, listen to them hum, like the
train tracks that run too close to our home.

I fold memories into wings of low flying birds,
amazed that the images talk to me still.

Each thing—

each stone, blossom, child—

is held in place.

Only we, in our arrogance,

push out beyond what we each belong to

for some empty freedom.

Rainer Maria Rilké

Sparrows Fly into the Kitchen

I develop a fear of closed doors,
men in endless white coats.
Watch a doctor with a limp
lean in to my mother.
Learn that war is punishment,
peace finer than a hair.

Some evenings my father
saves a space for us
tucked behind musings
of cars and fast women.
Infidelity like quicksand
fills his mouth.

In a room with sepia photographs
she paints transparent fish,
quotes Eliot and Yeats,
absorbs Byron's excesses,
studies Yoga, believes if she stands
on her head she will learn to forgive—

Sparrows fly into the kitchen
overwhelming her mind.
A wheeling of soft wings
into the dusk.

Rough Music

On quiet nights as the moon completes its arc
in the eyes of animals a soft white glow.
I remember her face looked like potatoes

buried too long under earth. Nursie Per Pursie sat
her fat bottom on the porcelain bath, blew bubbles
from palms of rough wrinkled hands. As a bubble

filled with rainbows floated up and away, she opened
a window into the night, murmured, *they hold dreams for
a child, help her forget why her mother isn't here.*

When lonely hours sear the spectre of silence
a surge of longing weeps through me.
I listen for my mother to walk the dark stairs.

The First Time We Lost Our House

There is a certain sharpness in the air
when the house fills with yells. I run past
waving foxgloves to a park down the road.

April offers us bluebells, primroses from her mouth.
There are six swings, a red rusty roundabout.
that chips in our hands.

The earth is giddy with bright flowers.
We discover a nest, a robin's blue egg.
The shell cracks. I peel it away.

Eyes stare blindly into the day.
Perhaps the earth will take it back
and part of me will get lost.

In a miasma of cherry blossoms
I struggle to breathe.
Feel life bend, break open the heart.

Sold Piano

My mother stopped singing around the house
the day Dad struck me with the back of his hand.

Over her shoulder air shimmered like a time of
forgetting. Why snow falls I begin to understand.

Last year, I ran from the man up the road who drank gin.
He became a stranger to himself a long time ago.

Watched as he coveted her prized possession,
Gran's antique piano with brass candlestick holders,

Handed her a check. Strange smile on his face.
We moved to a green home. Winter light on the floors.

Mum sewed curtains that billowed out of rusty French
doors. Whispered 'au revoir'. Waved us off to school.

As she wove her way through imperfect French phrases
I watched her bury her face in lonely white hands.

My mother understood the lining of the world,
how with impossible lightness snow rises in spring.

Thin Arms

She lives in fear, says the river chatters
like sparrows swooping at dusk, watches
dragonflies dance on the water's tight skin,
kingfishers dive for elegant striped bass.

The warning on the weir reads *danger, go no further.*
Her skirt floats wide like a sail in full wind,
hair heavy, weight of stones. Thin arms fall open.
Hair curls with a vengeance round the sign on the weir.

She hangs half naked like the bow sprit of a boat.
School children gather at the water's edge and blush.
A farmer cracks his whip, shatters the tension.
The smell of warm earth lifts under hoofs.

The water resembles a kind of dark satin.
A lone fisherman cuts auburn hair.
One slash of his knife.

Boys and Foxes

For Richard and Robert - the boys next door

The boys call a meeting in the tumbled down chicken coop.
Blue and brown speckled eggs snuggle under the bantams,
night time footprints of foxes cuddle the ground.

Feathers flat and wet squeeze their way into morning.
I place a stalk of hay between my teeth
as rain is shoveled out of the sky.

Last week I tiptoed through the copse behind our home,
branches hung heavy with dark imaginings.
A fox ran past, a hen flapped in its mouth.

My fear stayed inside me where I keep my voice.
From the distance of decades what will we say
about choices that made us who we became?

If we surrendered

to earth's intelligence

we could rise up rooted, like trees.

Rainer Maria Rilké

This Room

There is something
auspicious
about the moment
sunlight
slices a room.

One with eyes open
watches
light climb a wall
wonders
about her place—his place,

I Talk to Myself

I was born
to a romantic mother.
Aristocratic,
damaged by time

My father,
crippled by religion.
The seventh commandment
erased from his bible.

My parents
in innocence and anger
tore me
from my bearings.

All I have learned
takes me back to this.

How I danced in solitude,
walked alone.

First Knife

They were gentle at first.
Her head upon his shoulder,
until the first knife slashed canvas.

I carry their hollowness
on my hips,
in all angles within my body.

Know the humbleness of rain
that softens the edges of hours,
unlike minds— too far out of reach.

Woman to Madness

For seven winters she sat beside me,
snow on the ground.

We swung on the oak seat
her son had whittled.

It hung from silver chains
long enough to hang a man.

He built the tallest swing
I had ever seen.

Pushed me into
bone damp November.

My father had a way
of soothing the rain.

One day he forgot how to talk,
fell quiet halfway through a thought.

The gate closed.
The path excised behind me.

I stumbled into a woman
clutching at veils.

It is Impossible God is Close by when there is so much Memory in the World

I am a simple woman.
I do not require much happiness.
No light touches the water I sip.

What was it he said as he put me on the train?
I watched sunlight strike tracks,
like my mother's black moods

when the air went wild like an angered cat
uncontrollable, vicious.
Easier to let his daughter go!

My bones knocked together
seeking foothold,
searching for calm.

Is there something in the darkness that
wants to correct us?
Each time I think "yes" it answers "no".

Out of Tune

It is not a melody
when atonal music polishes
the nerves of people we love.

He stacked logs.
Green moss clung
to the side that faced north.

His arms bare,
blue eyes iridescent
like a kingfisher's throat.

The logs crackled and spit,
like his wife—
opened by violence—a long time ago.

Cup and Saucer

My world is an English meadow,
buttercups under chin,
the wide, black eyes of tidy sheep.
A dip into a valley,
that leads triumphant to a stream.

Hot wheels crunch gravel paths.
Swallows swoop sloping fields,
squared by hedges of hips and haws.
A snowy owl hoots from the roof
of an ancient thatched barn.

Heavy doors fly wide.
My brother's arms a harbor.
He slides a mismatched cup and saucer
across the table. Tea and ginger biscuits
waken our tongues.

Between the cloud's jagged edge
and the chestnut twig over there on the left,
I step entranced into his home.

Instead we entangle ourselves

in knots of our own making

struggle, lonely, confused.

Rainer Maria Rilké

Five in the Family

At three in the morning
there is no one to rescue you
in the quiet of night when the soul turns away.

A one eyed dog sniffs my shoes
travels with winter
to the end of the garden.

An effigy of Guy Fawkes
above a huge fire,
stirs thoughts of sixteen hundred and five.

A lit firework falls up my brother's
thick sleeve. Mum tears at his coat.
Buttons pop like wet corks.

The five of us family
for only seven more years.
Five worlds well met, part forever

into the fire,
into the night where time
lies shattered in the body of another.

I walk to the woods, cannot argue
with myself anymore about things
I thought I could understand.

Inhale the scent of blossoms
on a black thorn hedge, calmed
by the thought that each one offers new life.

A Single Bed

In an air conditioned room above Fifth Avenue,
the phone black in my hand.
A voice says, *your brother is dead.*

You who imagined the Seven Seas
on an upturned kitchen table,
dreamed a sheep farm in Australia.

In London the house shudders.
I think I might understand,
but your beige sweater hangs over a chair.

Hand prints smudge the wall where you stoked a fire.
You lie white in white satin,
have a light beard, a lover named Susan.

You climb stairs of marble.
Heavy doors close.
You will rest for a while on a single bed,

in the silver sheen and scale of silence,
filled with the weight of your shattered black bike.

Pressed Tin

We talk in tears, do not hear the rim of the hour.
A silver fish slaps against the tide.
I will not look into your eyes again.

Turn away as you lie dead on white satin
while the mother you loved so,
sets her dreams into stone.

A flag flaps like the sound of some
wounded pelican. On the wooden table
crushed grapes the color of blood.

In the village an old man sleeps rough on a bare
earthen floor. He would speak of adventures
but all the light has washed out of his bones.

A bucket hammered from gold differs
from one of pressed tin, unlike happiness
and unhappiness spun together in fire.

Three Miles to Totteridge Church

We sailed the oceans on long afternoon light,
draped in red shawls bought from gypsies
down the lane.

Horses seemed wide when we were eight and ten.
We rode out over meadows that stretched
beyond our home.

Ray shot a sparrow the day he turned fifteen.
We didn't lift our eyes to one another.
Dug a shallow grave.

He took me sailing on Grasmere Lake near Friars Crag,
strode ahead, our roles reversed.
I let him lead the way.

One day we stumbled into a field of Hereford bulls,
Ray said, *don't run, look straight ahead,*
reached back for my hand.

Now his cufflinks lie in the bottom of a drawer
with the necklace he gave me
when I turned seventeen.

I watched him waving slowly
the last time we said goodbye.
The syllables of sixteen Aprils stamped into our lives.

His friends walked three miles to Totteridge church.
Stood close to one another,
tried to ease their pain.

In a shady knoll under a rain washed granite stone,
dreams undreamt lie in ashes,
seep into the loam.

Teddy Bear, Teddy Bear

Sitting on the bed
belonged to my brother,
now he is dead.

While pain pries
with its stiff fingers
he whispers in my ear,
if you close
the doors of your heart

you will be unable
to hear the only life
you can save.

Dreams will float
out of reach,
memories come and go
like wind over water.
You will walk alone
in the dark night
of your soul.

My Brother Walks the Roof

My brother walks with care upon the roof.
We lived with a fever for life, nailed to earth.

The size of a child, he enters my room,
smells of lavender and soft blankets.

I kneel to live a while at the level of his eyes.
He lifts my whispers to his mouth.

I want things to shift—gather the words
of my brother, fill my mind with their sounds.

Wonder are the gifts he gives me from the grave
more profound, than the days he walked on earth?

The Other Photograph

I like the way autumn feels when it lies
like exhaustion all over a garden.

An album folded in blue faded silk
unravels like the life of our mother.

I remember a fire lit by you.
You are wearing your favorite brown sweater,

the one Mum knitted,
the one you wore *that* day.

Our little brother, hands tucked in pockets
tries to emulate you.

In puddles the reflections of sparrows and brothers
walking and talking on the rain slick road.

The sky a soft grey of birds turning on wing,
my mouth fills with echoes. A fire lit by you.

Elegy

Under an oak tree,
a Daphne bush
our parents
planted by his grave.

I'll trim the pink clover,
silver weed, thyme,
kneel and slide
my hands across his name.

So, like children, we begin again

to learn from things

because they are in God's heart;

they have never left him.

Rainer Maria Rilké

Unraveling

The ten thousand sounds
of the world fall to silence
as my mother struggles
to remember my name.

The sky lifts her in its arms,
opens a door for her to enter.

Unburdened by memory
the impartial scales of the moon
tip her into a bowl, with all
the lost words of the world.

Naked

Dad found her naked by the farmer's five bar gate
humming quietly to a field of cows. She told him
she didn't like music in her clothes. He phoned me
sobbing, asked me to come home.

When he opened the door Mum stood by his side where
she had stood for over sixty years. She had wound
a sweater hideously around long, thin legs. A string
of pearls swung from her bruised left arm.

A woman who quoted Shakespeare, Keats and Byron,
loved the cut of good clothes, resembled a scarecrow
in the middle of a field. Dad looked down, embarrassed.
Scrabble tiles scattered all over the floor.

Mum took a step towards me, a rare smile of recognition.
I buried my face in her hair before she could see tears.
We sat at the kitchen table. Watched rain fall on the pond,
in some preplanned sequence, easy on the eye.

Death

It was not her fault. Life should have
been tidy like houses in Bath
with trim Georgian windows.

Her anger ground me like fine glass
under square, low heels.

I learned to arrange my thoughts
around chrysanthemums
and the full moon.

Understood quickly about
beginnings and ends,
that the gods did not know me well.

Remember voices ricochet around a table,
the surprise of laughter,
the dusky smell of a late summer rose.

The quietness at midnight.
My mother, dead in my arms.

Violin

In the room
when my mother died
the image of
the peacemaker
flowed up slowly
like the stirring
of some violin
that has caught
just the right
shade of pain.

The essence
of this once
beautiful woman
drifted out
the open window—
feelings
resting still
in unspoken words.

Alpha and Omega

We watched my
mother's last breath lift
into the night
burdened by
the weight of
my father's name.

This is the door
through which
we enter and leave.
A force that whispers
we are in touch
with something real.

While the alpha
and omega
of wild flung skies
float without conscience
over the facts.

From Her Point of View

He asked how it was
in the room
when her Mother died.

She said
it was like
the birth of a butterfly.
Filled with love.
Unexpected.

Slow Turning

Three days after our father died
we met in the shadow of a bruise-colored sky.

Words were loud, washed over fields.
It was an hour when all the creatures cowed.

Dogs howled, horses dashed hooves,
lambs sought the comfort of mother's milk.

Cats left the warmth of the old Rayburn stove,
cattle stampeded to the corner of a field.

Then you built a silent wall.
The rusted five bar gate clangs shut.

Empty house! Taste of loss.
Slow turn to tears.

This is what the things can teach us:

to fall

patiently to trust our heaviness.

Even a bird has to do that

before he can fly.

Rainer Maria Rilké

Icicles

In her life
a woman is polished
once or twice
like fine silver.
In these moments
she shimmers.

In her restless bed,
no longer reflected
in the image of a man,
She thaws,
like the dripping
of icicles.

She owes
much to those
she no longer loves.
Leaving,
closes the door
gently.

Listen to the Silence

I watch my son's breath
lift above snow.
He is five.
There is nothing
that could ease his pain.
I do not say
a word about his father.
I do not owe that man a thing.
Understand now
what love can't forgive.

Across an icy pond
a leaf drifts,
like my life
blown off course.

In the stillness
my son whispers,
Mummy, listen to the silence.
I lift him.
The air becomes
indistinct with the winter.
Like a reflection
out of focus,
not quite able
to capture his eyes.

Divorce

In memory of Jerry

You said it was good luck to share stories over
matzo ball soup, pastrami on rye, Dr. Brown's soda,
vanilla ice cream.

There was still music in your soul
although you hid your heartache well.
We sat tall on three chairs pulled tight against earth,

wandered into the men's shop in the hotel.
You bought cashmere sweaters,
loving the way they felt in your hands.

I watched our boy throw his arms up to your waist.
His braces caught in the soft yellow wool.
You lifted him up, kissed his wet eyes.

Separation tugs at the least expected time.
I felt we were falling helpless and blind. Three chairs
set apart in this hard, new world.

Black Bag

Never until the last light breaks
will there be a night like that.
You ran out into the coal black,
cold black night, ran after
the blacker than coal black hearse,
into the weeping snow by the unmourning lake.

On a corner where branches hung low,
stood in full salute to this man you loved so
who lay cold and still
in a stiff black plastic bag,
zipped up in front of us so matter of fact.
Your cry from a place I dare not go.

You were his Aenaeas carrying Anchises
through the fires of Troy.
He left you three kisses Russian style,
left cheek then right, then left again.
Three chances to be close
in that long, blue body of light.

Unfinished

I think of how you
would have grown,
eyes like your brother's
hazel flecked with green.

I did not let you
cry out your first breath,
kiss your neck
speak your name.

You took part of me.
Who shares your secrets now?

On the wind
an unorthodox conversation.
Something about
the state of my soul.

Head in my hands
I kneel to the task.
Uncover that place
where the heart breaks apart.

Missing Hours

How do you find hours
that went missing?

I lean forward,
lift a bee from a web,

help it find its bearings,
rest it on the ground.

Sleeping

I inhabit mischief
in the harps
of Irish music,

the short parerga
in the trill
of the yellow billed cuckoo.

Do you see the copper coin
of sun that slips hungry
between the hills,

the heart
that beats beside you
sleeping still?

Last Request

I lose myself in worldly things. Taste the sweat
on the neck of my sure footed Arion,
ride him hard in the rasping surf near our home.

Before you left, you cut peonies
their blossoms falling open,
placed them on the table in my mother's blue vase.

It is quiet now you are gone.
I begin to understand.

While there is time I will savor the bronze
September sun, lie in perfect solitude
beneath an ageless Turner sky.

Beyond the lovely desolation of a wild Cornish peninsula
scatter my ashes on the mystic Irish sea.

You will hear a whisper
settle soft about your shoulders
fading in the darkness of the vast unknown.

To The Reader

I watch a bird land on
the white tablecloth of the sea.

There are no secrets
between us.

I lie on warm grass
absorbed in the dance,

think this is how we flow inward
how we push outward.

Standing slowly,
I reach inward.

Try to recall the rhythm
to walking on earth.

Over My Shoulder

Two kittens
stroke
the open door.

A sandpiper walks
like a lady
in high heels

as the spine
of the wind lies calm
across the bay.

The sun reflects
the image of a woman
bent so close

to that porous line.
She swims
in memories.

Combs her white hair
with a rhythm
all her own.

Notes

"How surely gravities law..." p 11

"Knots of our own making". The Book of Hours, 11, 16. Rainer Maria Rilké

Lullaby for a Baby Falling, p 13

During WWII everyone had to 'do their bit'. Men, after working during the day, were conscripted to work at night, some as Firemen.

Guns and the Dome, p 17

Ernie Pyle was a much loved English war correspondent during WWII. He inspired this poem.

St Paul's Cathedral, London was founded in AD 604. It sits at the highest point in London. The "Second Great Fire of London" refers to one of the most destructive air raids of the London Blitz. During the night of 29th December 1940 between 6pm and 6am more than 24,000 high explosive bombs and 100,000 incendiary bombs were dropped. St. Paul's caught fire and was put out by brave firemen many of whom lost their lives in the war.

Dress Walks Out the Door, p 19

English Red Cross nurses cared for the wounded in both WWI and WWII. After intensive training, many women helped to rehabilitate soldiers damaged by war while also holding down the fort at home. My Mother was one of these women.

Soft Curves, p 21

Until the end of the twentieth century in England, corporal punishment was still an acceptable form of discipline in public and private schools.

Rag and Bone, p 23

The 'Rag and Bone' man travelled through towns and villages. He would ring a bell and call out, "Any old rags and bones". Traditionally this was a task performed on foot with the scavenged materials (which included rags, bones and various metals) kept in a small bag slung over the shoulder. Some wealthier rag-and-bone men used a cart, sometimes pulled by horse or pony. 19th-century rag-and-bone men typically lived in penury, surviving on the proceeds of what they collected each day. Due in part to the soaring price of scrap metal, rag-and-bone men can once again be seen at work.

The last movement of Mahler's Fourth Symphony was written to expresses a child's vision of heaven.

"Each thing " p 25

Knots of Our Own Making, The Book of Hours, 11, 16. Rainer Maria Rilké

Rough Music, p 29

Nursie per Pursie was one of many nurses who cared for children when parents were unavailable because of injury, physical and emotional, or death during WWII.

"If we surrendered…" p 39

  Knots of Our Own Making, The Book of Hours 11,16. Rainer Maria Rilké

"Instead we entangle…"p 55

  Knots of Our Own Making, The Book of Hours 11,16. Rainer Maria Rilké

Five in the Family, p 57

  Guy Fawkes was a provincial English Catholic soldier. He fought in the Eighty Years War in Europe on the side of Catholic Spain. In 1605 he was an integral part of the plan to blow up the Houses of Parliament; caught, imprisoned, tried and sentenced to hang for his crime on January 31st, 1606, he jumped from the hanging tower and broke his neck.

Pressed Tin, p 61

  With many thanks to the poet Jane Hirshfield for the line from her poem, *Late Self Portrait by Rembrandt,* "Happiness and unhappiness/differ as a bucket hammered from gold differs from one of pressed tin…"

Three Miles to Totteridge Church p 63

  Totteridge Church is in the borough of Hertfordshire, England. There has been a church on this site since 1250 AD. The Yew tree in the grave yard is documented to be between one thousand and two thousand years of age.

Grasmere Lake is one of several notable lakes in the Lake District of the British Isles.

Elegy, p 71

The Daphne bush flowers from mid to late winter. The flowers are light and dark pink give off a beautiful fragrance.

"So, like children..." p 73

Knots of Our Own Making, <u>The Book of Hours</u> 11,16. Rainer Maria Rilké

Naked p 77, Slow Turning, p 87

A five bar gate is historically a farm gate used to sequester animals in fields. Tally marks, or hash marks, are a <u>unary numeral system</u> used for <u>counting</u>. In <u>Europe,</u> tally marks are most commonly written as groups of five lines. The first four lines are vertical, and every fifth line runs diagonally or horizontally across the previous four vertical lines, from the top of the first line, to the bottom of the fourth line (the popular direction may vary from region to region). The resulting mark is known as a five-bar gate.

Death, p 79

Georgian architecture is characterized by its proportion and balance, current between 1720 and 1840. Simple mathematical ratios were used to determine the height of a window in relation to its width or the shape of a room as a double cube.

"This is what things can teach us…" p 89

Knots of Our Own Making. The Book of Hours 11, 16.Rainer Maria Rilké

Black Bag, p 97

Anchises was a Trojan Prince and the father of Aeneas, the hero of Vergil's *Aeneid*. Anchises was crippled for revealing his coupling with the goddess Venus. This is told in *Aeneid* where he tries to talk his son into leaving him in Troy where he will surely die. When Aeneas left Troy, he carried his father to safety on his back.

Last Request, p 105

In Greek mythology, Arion or Areion was a divinely-bred, extremely swift immortal horse which, according to the Latin poet Sextus Propertius, was endowed with speech.

Joseph Mallord William Turner (23 April 1775- 19 December 1851) was an English Romantic landscape painter, watercolorist and printmaker, whose style can be said to have laid the foundation for Impressionism.

About the Author

Sarah has loved the music of words all her life. Raised by a mother who quoted poetry daily, Sarah devoured books from an early age. She grew up in London, kept a diary from the age of five. At twenty one Sarah immigrated to the United States. She worked as a stewardess for Pan American and travelled the world. After three years and in love, she moved to Hawaii where her son was born. He was riding tandem on her surf board from the age of two. Seven years later she began life anew in California. Sarah pursued her dream of returning to college. She obtained her B.A. in Anthropology from U.C.S.D. a Gemological Degree from the Gemological Institute of America and an M.F.A. in Creative Writing from S.D.S.U. She is trained as an instructor in the Amherst Writers Method and has studied Yoga from the age of seventeen. Sarah presently resides in California and Cornwall, England with her husband John, two cats, Leopold Bloom and Tse Wa (Tibetan for compassion). Her poems have been published in Avocet, California Anthology of Poets, the San Diego Review, The New Jersey Times, The Foundation for Women Celebration, Anthology of Creative Writing San Diego State University, Perigee Magazine, San Diego Poetry Annual, Foothill Journal of Poetry, 27 rue de fleures and other journals. *Over My Shoulder* is Sarah's first book of poetry and is dedicated to her family.